ISBN 978-1-5283-9222-8
PIBN 10980838

1 MONTH OF
FREE
READING

at
www.ForgottenBooks.com

By purchasing this book you are eligible for one month membership to ForgottenBooks.com, giving you unlimited access to our entire collection of over 1,000,000 titles via our web site and mobile apps.

To claim your free month visit:
www.forgottenbooks.com/free980838

ROPS AND MARKETS

VOLUME 59   NUMBER 12

E G G S (Page 276)

U. S. FOREIGN TRADE IN AGRICULTURAL PRODUCTS
(Page 280)

CONTENTS

FOR RELEASE

MONDAY

SEPTEMBER 19, 1949

Page

COTTON AND OTHER FIBER
Cotton-Price Quotations on Foreign Markets............ 299
FATS AND OILS .
Philippine August Copra Exports Largest in 1949...... 289
Ceylon Copra, Coconut Oil Exports Exceed 1948
Shipments... 290
U.S. Imports of Specified Vegetable Oils and Oilseeds 294
India Anticipates Larger Peanut, Castor, Sesame Crops 295
Vegetable Oilseeds and Oils Situation in Guatemala... 295
Malayan Copra Exports and Imports.................... 292
Malayan Coconut Oil Exports and Imports.............. 293
FRUITS, VEGETABLES AND NUTS
Canadian Fruit Estimate Revised...................... 300
GRAINS, GRAIN PRODUCTS AND FEEDS
Philippine Per Capita Rice Consumption Below Prewar. 285
Burma Maintains Rice Exports......................... 287
Panama Harvests Record Rice Crop..................... 287
Canada's Flour Milling Declines...................... 287
LIVESTOCK AND ANIMAL PRODUCTS
Indicated 1949 World Egg Production About 5 Percent
Above 1948 276
Livestock Numbers in Ireland Decrease................ 283
Danish Livestock Numbers, Except Horses, Increase
Substantially.. 284
Wool Prices 5 to 10 Percent Higher at Opening Sales
in Australia... 284
TROPICAL PRODUCTS
Indonesia's Pepper Production Continues Low.......... 297
Slightly Smaller Nigerian Cacao Production Forecast
For 1949-50.. 298

UNITED STATES DEPARTMENT OF AGRICULTURE
OFFICE OF FOREIGN AGRICULTURAL RELATIONS
WASHINGTON 25, D. C.

The Soviet Union and the Chinese Communists have concluded an agreement, valid for 1 year, under which the Chinese will export soybeans, vegetable oils, corn and rice to the Soviet Union in return for industrial equipment, motorcycles, crude oil, paper, medical instruments and medical supplies.

- - - - - -

That part of the currently proposed new British-Soviet Trade Agreement pertaining to grains is now in force although the over-all agreement has not yet been concluded. With respect to grains, the agreement provides for Soviet shipments to the United Kingdom of 500,000 metric tons of barley, 400,000 tons of corn and 100,000 tons of oats. Such shipments, if they materialize, will add substantially to the British feed supply. The previous agreement of December 1947 provided for 750,000 tons of coarse grains from the U.S.S.R., delivery of which was substantially fulfilled.

- - - - - -

Following the pattern already set in other British West African areas, the Gold Coast and Sierra Leone have also established separate Agricultural Produce Marketing Boards, to control the sale and export of specified agricultural commodities. In the case of the Gold Coast the agricultural items include coffee, oil palm produce, copra, coconut oil, shea nuts and shea butter. Cocoa is excluded since it is under control of a special Gold Coast Cocoa Marketing Board. The commodities under control in Sierra Leone are cocoa, coffee, copra, groundnuts and oil palm produce.

The objects of the two newly created Boards are identical to the other existing British West African marketing bodies, that is, buying crops from local producers at fixed prices and selling to overseas markets at prevailing world prices.

- - - - - -

(Continued on Page 300)

FOREIGN CROPS AND MARKETS

Published weekly to inform producers, processors, distributors and consumers of farm products of current developments abroad in the crop and livestock industries, foreign trends in prices and consumption of farm products, and world agricultural trade. Circulation of this periodical is free to those needing the information it contains in farming, business, and professional operations. Issued by the Office of Foreign Agricultural Relations of the U.S. Department of Agriculture, Washington 25, D.C.

INDICATED 1949 WORLD EGG PRODUCTION ABOUT 5 PERCENT ABOVE 1948

Egg production in 1949 in the principal producing countries for which reports were available appears approximately 5 percent above 1948, according to information available to the Office of Foreign Agricultural Relations. There have been important increases in production in the past year in western Europe, where the demand for eggs has been strong. More readily available feed supplies and favorable egg-feed price relationships have encouraged production. An increased rate of lay per hen in recent years has contributed to a larger world output of eggs.

Production in the United States thus far in 1949 has been almost the same as a year earlier and the total output for the year should differ little from 1948. Canada, on the other hand, continues to show a considerable decrease in egg production and is the only country where output is appreciably lower.

World egg production is about one-fifth above the 1934-38 prewar average. This is mainly accounted for by the 50 percent increase in the United States in the past 10 years. This sizeable increase heavily influences the world comparison as it represents a production 8 times larger than that of any other country and approximately one-half of all reported egg production.

Egg production in 1949 will exceed prewar in Belgium,Denmark, France, Sweden, and Switzerland, and favorable gains in production from low wartime levels were made in Ireland, the Netherlands, Czechoslovakia, and the United Kingdom. The countries now exporting eggs are led by Denmark, followed by Belgium, Ireland, the Netherlands, Hungary, and Belgium. Mediterranean European countries, on the other hand, have reported less pronounced increases in their egg production. Austria and Italy have shown a slight increase in production, while the output in Greece is below 1948.

Egg prices, almost without exception, have declined in 1949, but the increase in feed supplies has caused a more than comparable drop in the price of feed. Thus, in many countries, including the United States, the egg-feed ratio continues quite favorable. In addition to the increased availability of feed, the government supervision of hatcheries in many countries is gradually improving the quality of hens and contributing to the larger production of 1949.

The poultry industries of central and northwestern European countries, with the exception of the United Kingdom, have recovered to the extent that rationing and price controls are not the general rule. Many countries of this area have several broad programs, such as financing feed supplies, improving the quality of birds, supplying husbandry information, and providing sufficient inspection and market outlets.

EGGS 1/: Number produced in specified countries,
average 1934-38, annual 1946-1949

Countries	Average 1934-38	1946	1947	1948	Indicated 1949
	Millions	Millions	Millions	Millions	Millions
NORTH AMERICA					
Canada.................:	2,638	3,883	4,484	4,279	3,940
Panama................:	-	-	52	-	-
United States.........:	35,498	55,590	55,252	55,168	55,500
Cuba..................:	320	300	288	276	264
Dominican Republic....:	-	60	60	-	-
EUROPE					
Albania...............:	143	-	-	-	-
Austria...............:	663	270	285	350	380
Belgium...............:	1,693	1,100	1,380	1,440	1,800
Bulgaria..............:	682	-	-	-	-
Czechoslovakia........:	1,958	776	903	1,110	1,380
Denmark...............:	1,979	883	995	1,568	2,100
Eire..................:	1,086	801	733	920	1,080
Finland...............:	317	93	117	-	-
France................:	6,200	6,200	6,300	6,100	6,500
Germany...............:	6,585	-	-	-	-
Greece................:	550	349	376	367	350
Hungary...............:	1,050	-	650	750	-
Italy.................:	5,600	3,600	4,300	4,450	4,550
Luxembourg............:	40	-	30	35	35
Netherlands...........:	1,978	480	1,052	1,280	1,540
Norway................:	369	155	198	263	330
Poland and Danzig.....:	3,500	2,276	-	-	-
Portugal..............:	250	-	-	-	-
Rumania...............:	1,500	2/ 532	-	-	-
Spain.................:	1,700	-	1,992	1,800	-
Sweden................:	900	1,149	1,217	1,335	1,500
Switzerland...........:	423	391	442	520	599
United Kingdom - Farm 3/: 4/	3,871	2,418	2,600	3,000	3,500
Total 3/: 4/	5,098	3,850	4,000	4,300	5,000
Yugoslavia............:	1,000	-	-	-	-
ASIA					
Lebanon...............:	-	65	60	48	-
Palestine.............:	108	200	-	-	-
Syria.................:	92	120	90	110	-
Turkey................:	1,003	863	895	-	-
China.................:	-	-	-	-	-
Japan.................:	3,553	936	-	-	-
India.................:	-	2,794	-	-	-
Pakistan..............:	-	571	-	-	-
Philippine Islands....:	-	-	-	250	-
SOUTH AMERICA					
Argentina.............:	1,127	-	-	-	-
Brazil................:	-	-	-	2,160	-
Chile.................:	-	520	460	370	-
Paraguay..............:	-	-	100	-	-
Uruguay...............:	289	358	326	-	-
AFRICA					
Egypt.................:	751	-	-	-	-
French Morocco........:	1,000	-	-	-	-
Union of South Africa.:	5/	-	372	-	-
OCEANIA					
Australia 6/..........:	708	1,358	1,470	1,434	1,440
New Zealand...........:	430	-	-	-	-

1/ Relates to farm production in Canada and the United States, but data for many countries
not explicit on this point. 2/ 58 counties. 3/ Year ending in May of year indicated.
4/ 3-year average. 5/ Not available. 6/ Commercial production.

Office of Foreign Agricultural Relations. Prepared or estimated on the basis of official
statistics of foreign governments, reports of United States Foreign Service officers, results
of office research, and other information. Data relate to prewar boundaries, unless other-
wise noted.

The lowland countries, Denmark, the Netherlands, and Belgium, have all resumed exports. Denmark will produce, consume and export more eggs this year than in 1948. The imports of grains and the reduced price of poultry feed provide farmers with an optimistic outlook, since considerable export markets have been obtained. Danish farmers will tend to increase egg production under egg-feed relationships as favorable as those currently prevailing. Domestic consumption of eggs has been 10 percent higher than prewar due to the meat shortage, but high prices will cause more to be sold and less to be eaten at home. Danish efforts to provide high quality products in ample supply have boosted their eggs to third place in national export.

Higher egg production in the Netherlands this year has enabled exports to be resumed at an important level, but current levels have been reached by requiring a portion of each poultryman's egg delivery for export in order to provide exchange credits to purchase the necessary protein feeds for the poultry industry. The Netherlands has removed rationing and in February dropped price controls. This has permitted consumers to bid freely for their egg supplies at a price which is profitable to poultrymen. Few eggs were placed in·storage in 1949. The largest hatch since the war occurred in 1949.

Belgium returned to an egg export basis in April and the government has been enforcing quality controls so that only high-grade eggs will leave the country. Egg prices have declined but are in favorable relation to feed due to the larger feed supplies from both indigenous and foreign sources. As yet, the rate of lay per hen has been fairly low as a result of diseases and overcrowded poultry houses.

In 1948, egg production in Ireland increased substantially during sub-sidization from the United Kingdom and the Irish governments. This governmental aid has decreased in 1949, but the prices offered remain favorable enough so that definite expansion in egg production is encouraged. The Irish hope that the result of negotiations with England will be the continuance of price-setting two years in advance for unlimited quantities of exports, thus permitting forward planning by farmers. High quality chicks were offered at low prices during the hatching season by the government, enabling the farmers to increase the rate of lay.

In 1949 egg production in the United Kingdom increased as a result of favorable weather and some increase in chicken numbers. Feed supplies are furnished in proportion to egg deliveries to packing stations and are more abundant than formerly. Norway is still in short supply and unable to meet domestic requirements. Egg production is profitable and conditions are quite favorable for poultrymen. The large hatch in 1949 is expected to ease the shortage by the end of the year.

Sweden appears to have ample egg supplies. However, the low government support price in 1949 is expected to discourage a large hatch this year. The present high level of consumer purchasing and the continuation of meat rationing are expected to assist in maintaining a strong domestic egg market. Further increases in Swedish egg production would necessitate seeking foreign market outlets.

Egg production in France is now about 5 percent above prewar. Chicken numbers equal or exceed prewar and grain prices are generally favorable to feeding for a relatively high rate of lay. Farmers can now buy and sell secondary cereals without transportation and end use permits. Notwithstanding a higher egg production in France than prewar, supplies to consumers in urban centers are not always obtainable at reasonable prices.

The Mediterranean countries seem to be generally less concerned about their poultry industries and have administered less effective poultry programs. These countries are still heavy importers of eggs and also import feed for domestic production and continue to operate rationing and delivery production programs.

Czechoslovakian egg production, while still materially below prewar, has recovered somewhat from a low wartime level. Egg production has been facilitated by government control of hatcheries that have offered more and better chicks. This, plus the aid of improved feed supplies, should considerably ease the demand for eggs by this fall. The recently revised requirements for egg deliveries are based upon the number of hectares in each farm and not on the number of poultry as was the previous plan.

Austria received urgently needed feed imports through the assistance of ECA, which may increase egg production. Larger domestic production and imports are needed to ease the black market trade in eggs.

Greece has continued to decrease its egg production due mainly to continued spread of Newcastle disease and the lack of concentrated feeds. High import duties on feed and no duty on eggs make it easier to import eggs than to remove domestic production difficulties.

South American governments are giving more attention than in the past to encouragement of egg production but outside of Venezuela the efforts are not important, since the poultry industries of the other countries consist mostly of very small native flocks. Large commercial poultry enterprises with modern production and marketing methods are being encouraged in Venezuela.

In Argentina, Uruguay, and Chile, the 1949 feed supplies have been more plentiful and the egg production outlook appears favorable.

The Canadian production of farm eggs in 1949 will be about 330 million less than last year. Chicken numbers have continued below 1948 in spite of the 15 percent increase in hatch during 1949 over 1948.

The increased demand for chicks was relatively greater for cockerels of heavier breeds than for pullets. This change in interest results from the doubtful egg export market in 1950. Currently, the egg-feed ratio is relatively favorable.

The United States production in the first half of 1949 was slightly below the same period in 1948. The decrease was due to a smaller national flock and possibly to a larger carryover of hens. In the remaining months, however, the expected addition of pullets from the large 1949 hatch may yield an increase in production of eggs in 1949 over 1948. The present egg-feed ratio should encourage heavier feeding which would raise the rate of lay slightly.

This is one of a series of regularly scheduled reports on world agricultural production approved by the Office of Foreign Agricultural Relations Committee on Foreign Crop and Livestock Statistics. For this report, the Committee was composed of Arthur W. Palmer, Acting Chairman, Floyd E. Davis, Charles C. Wilson, and Stanley Mehr.

U. S. FOREIGN TRADE IN AGRICULTURAL PRODUCTS DURING JULY 1949

On a value basis, United States exports of agricultural products during July, the first month of the fiscal year 1949-50, amounted to $235,000,000, a level substantially lower than that for any month during the entire two preceding years.

In July 1948, agricultural exports were valued at $278,000,000. The monthly average for all of 1948-49 was $319,000,000 compared with $292,000,000 in 1947-48. Wheat and flour continued in first place although the value of the exports was substantially lower than in July a year ago. Cotton continued to hold second place in value.

On a quantitative basis, the outstanding features of the July exports this year were the large increases in exports of lard, tallow, apples and pears, corn, rice, peanuts, soybeans and soybean oil compared with those for July 1948 and the large reduction in exports of citrus fruit, dried fruit, wheat and wheat flour, tobacco, soya flour and dried peas.

United States imports of agricultural products during July 1949 were valued at $205,000,000 compared with $239,000,000 in July 1948. The monthly average for all of 1948-49 was $250,000,000 compared with $239,000,000 during 1947-48. Coffee, sugar, crude rubber and wool continued to head the list. On a quantitative basis, the outstanding features shown by the July import figures are the large increases in imports of coffee, copra, coconut oil, palm oil and barley malt compared with those for July 1948 and the large reductions in imports of crude rubber, wool, tung oil, molasses, hides and skins and canned beef.

UNITED STATES: Summary of exports, domestic, of selected
agricultural products during July, 1948 and 1949

Commodity exported	:Unit:	July			
		Quantity		Value	
		1948	1949	1948	1949
				1,000	1,000
ANIMAL PRODUCTS:		:Thousands	:Thousands	dollars	:dollar
Butter..........................	Lb.:	319	295	292	20
Cheese..........................	Lb.:	7,331	18,061	3,586	6,45
Milk, condensed.................	Lb.:	10,886	6,205	2,186	1,26
Milk, whole, dried.............	Lb.:	9,387	5,499	5,084	2,76
Nonfat dry milk solids.........	Lb.:	9,674	2,857	1,539	40
Milk, evaporated...............	Lb.:	21,650	22,967	3,383	2,97
Eggs, dried....................	Lb.:	95	2,582	113	2,44
Beef and veal, total 1/	Lb.:	1,073	1,482	475	45
Pork, total 1/	Lb.:	1,649	6,102	826	2,16
Horse meat.....................	Lb.:	10,523	2,613	1,744	40
Lard (incl. neutral)...........	Lb.:	20,747	52,293	5,315	7,02
Tallow, edible and inedible....		6,453	24,740	1,194	1,97
VEGETABLE PRODUCTS:					
Cotton,unmfd.excl. linters (480 lb.)..	:Bale:	155	232	27,605	38,57
Apples, fresh..................	Lb.:	948	5,479	82	32
Grapefruit, fresh..............	Lb.:	12,798	3,891	397	19
Oranges, fresh.................	Lb.:	51,083	31,100	1,780	1,70
Pears, fresh...................	Lb.:	34	3,053	5	31
Prunes, dried..................	Lb.:	6,794	1,703	543	22
Raisins and currants...........	Lb.:	12,947	1,862	1,142	20
Fruits, canned.................	Lb.:	2,689	6,307	410	79
Fruit juices...................	:Gal.:	1,343	1,445	809	1,25
Barley, grain (48 lb.).........	Bu.:	1,163	3,981	2,867	5,45
Barley malt (34 lb.)..........	Bu.:	541	218	1,775	45
Corn, grain (56 lb.)..........	Bu.:	498	8,881	1,159	14,45
Grain sorghums (56 lb.).......	Bu.:	2,125	5,360	5,171	7,59
Rice, milled, brown, etc......	Lb.:	7,663	86,187	970	6,77
Wheat, grain (60 lb.).........	Bu.:	32,748	24,789	92,130	58,13
Flour, wholly of U.S. wheat (100 lb.).:	Bag:	6,725	2,615	48,232	12,74
Flour, other (100 lb.)........	Bag:	27	392	204	2,17
Hops..........................	Lb.:	192	167	170	9
Peanuts, shelled..............	Lb.:	5,822	34,724	1,059	3,78
Soybeans (except canned)......	Lb.:	1,324	73,200	123	3,04
Soybean oil, crude and refined.......	Lb.:	3,182	46,229	839	6,31
Soya flour....................	Lb.:	75,419	111	5,030	
Seeds, field and garden.......	Lb.:	890	386	240	15
Tobacco leaf, bright flue-cured.......	Lb.:	53,154	20,420	26,704	8,65
Tobacco leaf, other...........	Lb.:	5,420	10,015	3,089	5,19
Beans, dried..................	Lb.:	5,714	4,928	739	48
Peas, dried...................	Lb.:	24,035	1,570	2,036	11
Potatoes, white...............	Lb.:	15,459	10,468	544	35
Vegetables, canned............	Lb.:	4,915	5,062	805	79
Total above...................				252,396	209,01
Food exported for relief, etc.........				1,629	71
Other agricultural products...........				24,353	25,06
Total agricultural............				278,378	234,85
Total all commodities.........				1,010,019	886,71

1/ Product weight. Compiled from official records of the Bureau of the Census.

UNITED STATES: Summary of imports for consumption
of selected agricultural products during July, 1948 and 1949

Commodity imported SUPPLEMENTARY	Unit	July			
		Quantity		Value	
		1948	1949	1948	1949
		Thousands	Thousands	1,000 dollars	1,000 dollars
MALS AND ANIMAL PRODUCTS:					
tle, dutiable......................	No.	12:	23:	1,810	3,656
tle, free (for breeding)...........	No.	5:	1:	1,163	339
ein and lactarene.................	Lb.	5,878:	948:	1,373	127
ese...............................	Lb.	1,491:	2,206:	792	1,147
les and skins.....................	Lb.	22,339:	13,280:	9,845	5,890
f canned, incl. corned............	Lb.	18,148:	11,524:	5,924	3,740
l, unmfd.,excl. free, etc.........	Lb.	29,699:	12,957:	16,660	8,284
ETABLES PRODUCTS:					
ton,unmfd.,excl.linters (480 lb.).	Balo	8:	11:	1,332	1,258
te and jute butts,unmfd.(2,240 lb.):	Ton	9:	55:	3,303	290
ples, green or ripe (50 lb.).......	Bu.	0:	2:	0	5
ives in brine.....................	Gal.	1,052:	366:	1,642	822
ieapples, prep. or preserved......	Lb.	15,838:	11,193:	2,140	1,346
rley malt.........................	Lb.	990:	8,466:	78	426
ps................................	Lb.	14:	1:	16	1
monds, shelled....................	Lb.	460:	58:	157	19
azil or cream nuts, not shelled....	Lb.	1,607:	1,029:	221	102
show nuts.........................	Lb.	3,088:	2,815:	1,183	1,142
conut meat, shredded, etc.........	Lb.	8,086:	11,519:	2,003	1,717
stor beans........................	Lb.	15,153:	11,667:	1,023	559
pra...............................	Lb.	49,832:	55,817:	7,052	4,023
axseed (56 lb.)...................	Bu.	332:	0:	1,946	0
conut oil.........................	Lb.	2,991:	14,512:	692	1,864
lm oil............................	Lb.	2,329:	12,922:	476	1,735
ng oil............................	Lb.	12,810:	2,301:	2,513	378
gar,excl. beet (2,000 lb.)........	Ton	238:	365:	22,470	36,525
lasses, unfit for human consumption:	Gal.	14,064:	7,771:	2,720	311
bacco, cigarette leaf.............	Lb.	4,848:	4,581:	3,867	3,394
bacco, other leaf................	Lb.	1,179:	1,535:	1,744	2,103
tatoes, white....................	Lb.	619:	5,054:	15	113
matoes, fresh....................	Lb.	43:	48:	3	2
COMPLEMENTARY					
ol, unmfd., free in bond..........	Lb.	31,478:	10,124:	8,482	3,387
ETABLE PRODUCTS:					
nanas.............................	Bunch	4,959:	5,033:	4,266	5,178
ffee (ex. into Puerto Rico).......	Lb.	184,339:	222,288:	50,357	58,432
coa or cacao beans and shells.....	Lb.	47,243:	48,933:	15,611	8,337
a.................................	Lb.	7,360:	6,129:	3,693	2,046
ices (complementary)..............	Lb.	5,296:	6,064:	2,149	2,761
sal and henequen (2,240 lb.)......	Ton	10:	7:	3,201	1,837
bber, crude......................	Lb.	142,965:	103,459:	27,233	16,649
Total above......................				209,155	179,945
her agricultural products.........				29,409	25,201
Total agricultural...............				238,564	205,146
Total all commodities............				567,981	458,030

mpiled from official records of the Bureau of the Census.

UNITED STATES: Summary of exports, domestic, of selected
agricultural products during July, 1948 and 1949

Commodity exported	:Unit:	July			
		Quantity		Value	
		1948	1949	1948	1949
		1,000 :Thousands	1,000 :Thousands	1,000 dollars	1,000 dollars
ANIMAL PRODUCTS:					
Butter....	Lb.:	319	295	292	201
Cheese....	Lb.:	7,331	18,061	3,586	6,453
Milk, condensed....	Lb.:	10,886	6,205	2,186	1,265
Milk, whole, dried....	Lb.:	9,387	5,499	5,084	2,762
Nonfat dry milk solids....	Lb.:	9,674	2,857	1,539	403
Milk, evaporated....	Lb.:	21,650	22,967	3,383	2,976
Eggs, dried....	Lb.:	95	2,582	113	2,447
Beef and veal, total 1/	Lb.:	1,073	1,482	475	455
Pork, total 1/	Lb.:	1,649	6,102	826	2,166
Horse meat....	Lb.:	10,523	2,613	1,744	408
Lard (incl. neutral)....	Lb.:	20,747	52,293	5,315	7,027
Tallow, edible and inedible....	Lb.:	6,453	24,740	1,194	1,977
VEGETABLE PRODUCTS:					
Cotton,unmfd.excl. linters (480 lb.)..	:Bale:	155	232	27,605	38,573
Apples, fresh....	Lb.:	948	5,479	82	326
Grapefruit, fresh....	Lb.:	12,798	3,891	397	192
Oranges, fresh....	Lb.:	51,083	31,100	1,780	1,705
Pears, fresh....	Lb.:	34	3,053	5	319
Prunes, dried....	Lb.:	6,794	1,703	543	229
Raisins and currants....	Lb.:	12,947	1,862	1,142	204
Fruits, canned....	Lb.:	2,689	6,307	410	792
Fruit juices....	Gal.:	1,343	1,445	809	1,258
Barley, grain (48 lb.)....	Bu.:	1,163	3,981	2,867	5,450
Barley malt (34 lb.)....	Bu.:	541	218	1,775	497
Corn, grain (56 lb.)....	Bu.:	498	8,881	1,159	14,498
Grain sorghums (56 lb.)....	Bu.:	2,125	5,360	5,171	7,594
Rice, milled, brown, etc....	Lb.:	7,663	86,187	970	6,777
Wheat, grain (60 lb.)....	Bu.:	32,748	24,789	92,130	58,137
Flour, wholly of U.S. wheat (100 lb.).:	Bag:	6,725	2,615	48,232	12,745
Flour, other (100 lb.)....	Bag:	27	392	204	2,176
Hops....	Lb.:	192	167	170	94
Peanuts, shelled....	Lb.:	5,822	34,724	1,059	3,782
Soybeans (except canned)....	Lb.:	1,324	73,200	123	3,042
Soybean oil, crude and refined....	Lb.:	3,182	46,229	839	6,319
Soya flour....	Lb.:	75,419	111	5,030	6
Seeds, field and garden....	Lb.:	890	386	240	157
Tobacco leaf, bright flue-cured....	Lb.:	53,154	20,420	26,704	8,698
Tobacco leaf, other....	Lb.:	5,420	10,015	3,089	5,191
Beans, dried....	Lb.:	5,714	4,928	739	481
Peas, dried....	Lb.:	24,035	1,570	2,036	110
Potatoes, white....	Lb.:	15,459	10,468	544	326
Vegetables, canned....	Lb.:	4,915	5,062	805	798
Total above....				252,396	209,016
Food exported for relief, etc....				1,629	771
Other agricultural products....				24,353	25,068
Total agricultural....				278,378	234,855
Total all commodities....				1,010,019	886,746

1/ Product weight. Compiled from official records of the Bureau of the Census.

UNITED STATES: Summary of imports for consumption
of selected agricultural products during July, 1948 and 1949

Commodity imported SUPPLEMENTARY	Unit	July			
		Quantity		Value	
		1948	1949	1948	1949
				1,000	1,000
ANIMALS AND ANIMAL PRODUCTS:		Thousands	Thousands	dollars	dollars
Cattle, dutiable...................	No.	12:	23:	1,810	3,656
Cattle, free (for breeding)..........	No.	5:	1:	1,163	339
Casein and lactarene..............	Lb.	5,878:	948:	1,373	127
Cheese............................	Lb.	1,491:	2,206:	792	1,147
Hides and skins...................	Lb.	22,339:.	13,280:	9,845	5,890
Beef canned, incl. corned..........	Lb.	18,148:	11,524:	5,924	3,740
Wool, unmfd.,excl. free,.etc........	Lb.	29,699:	12,957:	16,660	8,284
VEGETABLES PRODUCTS:.					
Cotton,unmfd.,excl.linters (480 lb.).	Bale	8:	11:	1,332	1,258
Jute and jute butts,unmfd.(2,240 lb.)	Ton	9:	55:	3,303	290
Apples, green or ripe (50 lb.).......	Bu.	0:	2:	0	5
Olives in brine.......................	Gal.	1,052:	366:	1,642	822
Pineapples, prep. or preserved.......	Lb.	15,838:	11,193:	2,140	1,346
Barley malt........................	Lb.	990:	8,466:	78	426
Hops..............................	Lb.	14:	1:	16	1
Almonds, shelled....................	Lb.	460:	58:	157	19
Brazil or cream nuts, not shelled....	Lb.	1,607:	1,029:	221	102
Cashew nuts........................	Lb.	3,088:	2,815:	1,183	1,142
Coconut meat, shredded, etc..........	Lb.	8,086:	11,519:	2,003	1,717
Castor beans.......................	Lb.	15,153:	11,667:	1,023	559
Copra.............................	Lb.	49,832:	55,817:	7,052	4,023
Flaxseed (56 lb.)....................	Bu.	332:	0:	1,946	0
Coconut oil........................	Lb.	2,991:	14,512:	692	1,864
Palm oil...........................	Lb.	2,329:	12,922:	476	1,735
Tung oil...........................	Lb.	12,810:	2,301:	2,513	378
Sugar,excl. beet (2,000 lb.).........	Ton	238:	365:	22,470	36,525
Molasses, unfit for human consumption	Gal.	14,064:	7,771:	2,720	311
Tobacco, cigarette leaf..............	Lb.	4,848:	4,581:	3,867	3,394
Tobacco, other leaf................	Lb.	1,179:	1,535:	1,744	2,103
Potatoes, white....................	Lb.	619:	5,054:	15	113
Tomatoes, fresh....................	Lb.	43:	48:	3	2
COMPLEMENTARY					
Wool, unmfd., free in bond..........	Lb.	31,478:	10,124:	8,482	3,387
VEGETABLE PRODUCTS:					
Bananas...........................	Bunch	4,959:	5,033:	4,266	5,178
Coffee (ex. into Puerto Rico)........	Lb.	184,339:	222,288:	50,357	58,432
Cocoa or cacao beans and shells......	Lb.	47,243:	48,933:	15,611	8,337
Tea...............................	Lb.	7,360:	6,129:	3,693	2,046
Spices (complementary)..............	Lb.	5,296:	6,064:	2,149	2,761
Sisal and henequen (2,240 lb.).......	Ton	10:	7:	3,201	1,837
Rubber, crude......................	Lb.	142,965:	103,459:	27,233	16,649
Total above.....................				209,155	179,945
Other agricultural products..........				29,409	25,201
Total agricultural..............				238,564	205,146
Total all commodities...........				567,981	458,030

Compiled from official records of the Bureau of the Census.

```
┌──────────────────────────────────────────┐
│  C O M M O D I T Y   D E V E L O P M E N T S  │
└──────────────────────────────────────────┘
```

LIVESTOCK AND ANIMAL PRODUCTS

LIVESTOCK NUMBERS IN
IRELAND INCREASE

    Livestock numbers in Ireland for the 3 principal species showed a slight increase on January 1, 1949 over a year earlier. Cattle and sheep numbers were only about 2 percent above the preceding year. This places cattle numbers at a little above the prewar level and sheep about 28 percent below. Hog numbers, however, registered the largest gain and were 38 percent above the January 1948 numbers, but are still approximately 38 percent below their prewar level. These increases represent the prevailing optimism in the domestic livestock industry, reflecting a favorable feed situation and prices sufficiently satisfactory to encourage a larger output.

IRELAND: Livestock numbers on January 1, 1949,
with comparisons

Classification	1939	1946	1947	1948	1949
	:Thousands	:Thousands	:Thousands	:Thousands	:Thousands
Cattle					
Milk cows............	1,243	1,201	1,166	1,126	1,123
Heifers in calf.......	121	108	143	120	152
Bulls................	21	25	21	20	20
Other cattle:					
3 years and over.....	132	296	252	257	310
2-3 years...........	502	709	636	635	619
1-2 years...........	730	875	740	713	678
Under 1 year.........	837	932	745	660	703
Total cattle.......	3,586	4,146	3,703	3,531	3,605
Hogs					
Sows for breeding.....	94	48	47	40	59
Boars................	2	1	1	1	1
Pigs:					
Under 3 months.......	357	233	191	146	237
3 months and over....	367	197	215	183	213
Total hogs.......	820	479	454	370	510
Sheep					
Ewes for breeding.....	1,412	1,001	1,034	939	977
Rams................	62	35	43	41	42
Other sheep:					
1 year and over......	(820	(1,387	374	349	354
Under 1 year.........	(	(	329	297	287
Total sheep........	2,294	2,423	1,780	1,626	1,660

Compiled from Official Sources.

DANISH LIVESTOCK NUMBERS, EXCEPT
HORSES, INCREASE SUBSTANTIALLY

Cattle numbers in Denmark in July, according to the estimates of the
Danish Statistical Department, were almost 5 percent larger than a year
earlier. Milk cows showed an increase of nearly 4.5 percent over July 1948.
Total cattle numbers, however, are still below the level immediately following the war and are 11 percent smaller than prewar. Hog numbers, ob-
viously, showed the largest gain of about 84 percent (a correction from
102 percent indicated in the August 22, 1949 issue of Foreign Crops and
Markets), with bred sow numbers increasing about 78 percent over a year
earlier. Horse numbers, on the other hand, decreased by almost 8 percent from the preceding year and are now about 11 percent below prewar.
Chicken numbers in July were about 7.5 percent larger than July 1948.
The various increases reflect more adequate feed supplies, somewhat
larger domestic consumption, and considerable increase in export demand,
particularly for bacon.

DENMARK: Livestock and poultry numbers on
July 16, 1949, with comparisons

Classification	Average 1936-40	Average 1941-45	1946	1947	1948	1949
	Thousands	Thousands	Thousands	Thousands	Thousands	Thousands
Cattle, total......	3,227	3,087	3,167	3,014	2,826	2,962
Milk cows.........	1,625	1,500	1,594	1,546	1,472	1,537
Hogs, total........	3,200	1,808	1,768	1,830	1,462	2,690
Sows, total.......	368	212	191	206	202	362
Horses............	579	626	653	601	573	528
Chickens..........	27,832	14,447	18,338	19,415	23,445	25,199

Compiled from Official Sources.

CORRECTION

United Kingdom hog numbers, on page 233 of Foreign Crops and Markets,
of September 5, 1949, should have read 2,811,000 head for 1949 rather than
2,181,000.

WOOL PRICES 5 TO 10 PERCENT HIGHER
AT OPENING SALES IN AUSTRALIA

The 1949-50 Australian wool selling season opened August 29 with
competition unusually strong on the part of England and the Continent.
United States and Australian interests were cautious and contributed
little to the bidding.

Approximately 100,000 bales were offered at the Sydney and Adelaide sales. Clearance was good and prices 5 to 10 percent higher than the June closings were realized. Some observers believed that buyers were operating under "buy-at-best-price" orders.

The higher openings was expected by most observers in view of the short supply position and the high rate of consumption. In the interim between the June closing and the August openings, a strong spot market developed in Bradford, markets in South America became active, and even the crutchings sales in New Zealand showed strength.

Raw wool is needed to fill immediate demands and prices are expected to remain high in the near future.

GRAINS, GRAIN PRODUCTS AND FEEDS

PHILIPPINE PER CAPITA RICE
CONSUMPTION BELOW PREWAR

Per capita consumption of milled rice by Philippine consumers in 1949 is estimated at 17 percent below the prewar average (1936-40), according to official information transmitted by the American Embassy, Manila. The consumption rate has been rising since 1946, when it dropped 35 percent as the result of World War II. The reason it has remained below prewar in 1949, however, apparently is not because availabilities are less, but because the population has increased faster than supplies. Both the 1948-49 crop and 1949 imports have been larger than before the war.

PHILIPPINES: Consumption of milled rice, per rice consumer, averages 1926-40, annual 1946-49

Year	Net food supply 1/	Population		Per capita per rice consumer	
		Total	Rice consuming 2/	Annual	Daily
	Million pounds	Million	Million	Pounds	Ounces
Average					
1926-30............:	2,936	12.5	8.7	334	14.6
1931-35............:	2,887	14.0	9.8	292	12.8
1936-40............:	3,004	15.7	11.0	270	11.9
1946..............:	2,387	18.3	12.8	185	7.8
1947..............:	2,645	18.7	13.1	201	8.8
1948..............:	2,789	19.2	13.4	205	8.8
1949 3/...........:	3,145	19.6	13.7	229	9.9

1/ Production plus exports less seed, feed, waste and exports. 2/ Seventy percent of the Philippine population. 3/ Estimated.

Compiled in the American Embassy from data of the Bureau of Census and Statistics.

Despite plans to increase production in 1949-50, the planted acreage is about the same as in the year before. The rice area is forecast at 5,250,000 acres compared with 5,267,000 acres in 1948-49 and with the average of 4,934,000 acres before the war (1936-37/40-41). Lack of rainfall during the seeding period was the most important factor preventing an increase, and infestation of army and cut worms more serious than usual destroyed part of the upland rice and seedlings to be transplanted.

Rice imports into the Philippines during the first half of 1949 totaled 188 million pounds from the following countries (million pounds): United States, 82; Siam, 78; and Burma, 28. Total allocations of the International Emergency Food Council to be imported during 1949 are 298 million pounds, from the following countries of origin (million pounds): United States, 104; Siam, 54; Burma, 54; Ecuador, 44; Egypt, 22; and Brazil, 21.

Wholesale prices of domestic rice during 1949 have remained at a relatively high level. Quotations during the first four weeks of August were from $11.34 to $11.54 per 100 pounds compared with $12.96 to $13.16 per 100 pounds in the first week of August a year earlier, the only week when prices were quoted. Imported rice from the United States in August sold at from $9.37 to $9.84 per 100 pounds. The rough rice price to producers from January through August 27 held at $3.02 per bushel.

PHILIPPINES: Rice prices, per 100 pounds, August 1-27, 1949, with comparisons

Date	Native Macan milled ex-warehouse Manila		Imported	Rough rice delivered Cabanatuan
	No. 1	No. 2		
	Dollars	Dollars	Dollars	Dollars
1948				
August 2-7, High....	13.36	13.16	1/ 11.43	8.57
August 2-7, Low.....	13.36	12.96	1/ 11.43	8.57
1949				
January-High........	11.14	11.14	13.21	6.70
January-Low.........	10.77	10.53	11.43	6.70
February-High.......	11.34	11.14	11.43	6.70
February-Low........	10.77	10.53	11.43	6.70
March-High..........	11.34	11.14	11.43	6.70
March-Low...........	11.06	10.85	11.43	6.70
April-High..........	11.34	11.14	11.43	6.70
April-Low...........	11.14	10.93	11.43	6.70
May-High............	11.34	11.14	11.43	6.70
May-Low.............	11.14	10.93	9.66	6.70
June-High...........	12.15	11.94	2/ 9.07	6.70
June-Low............	11.14	11.26	8.85	6.70
July-High...........	3/	11.74	4/ 10.30	6.70
July-Low............	3/	11.34	2/ 8.85	6.70
August 1-27-High....	3/	11.54	4/ 9.84	6.70
August 1-27-Low.....	3/	11.34	4/ 9.37	6.70

1/ Siam, 5-10 percent broken. 2/ Egyptian. 3/ Unquoted. 4/ United States rice.

Daily Market Report, Bureau of Commerce, Philippine Government.

Although rice is the main food of 70 percent of the Philippine population, according to official data, the lower per capita disappearance of rice is not necessarily indicative of an acute shortage of foodstuffs. In 1945 and 1946 the United States Army distributed a large volume of food among the population. Consumption of domestic root crops has been considerably higher than before the war, and imports of flour and several other foods almost double the prewar average.

BURMA MAINTAINS
RICE EXPORTS

Burma's rice exports in August totaled 218 million pounds, bringing January-August shipments to 2,145 million pounds. In July 224 million pounds were shipped and exporters hope to deliver around 150 million pounds in September. The 1948 exports totaled 2,725 million pounds.

PANAMA HARVESTS
RECORD RICE CROP

Panama's record rice harvest of 1949 is forecast at 3,917,000 bushels (115 million pounds milled) compared with the preceding year's crop of 3,691,000 bushels (108 million pounds) and with the prewar (1935-39) average of 1,600,000 bushels (47 million pounds). Harvesting began in the last week of August. Panama's rice consumption in 1948 was around 120 million pounds of milled rice, of which 12 million were imported.

CANADA'S FLOUR
MILLING DECLINES

Canadian wheat flour production for the year ended July 31, 1949 declined to 20.3 million barrels, compared with 24.2 million barrels in 1947-48 and the record grind of 28.6 million in 1946-47. The low output in the season just ended was the smallest since 1941-42.

Wheat millings were smaller than a year earlier throughout the season, with the smallest figure reported for July 1949. That month's millings for flour were reported at 6.4 million bushels, compared with 8.4 million bushels for July 1948, and represent the smallest single month's production since June 1942.

Customs exports of wheat flour during the year ended July 1949 are indicated to be about 48 million bushels in grain equivalent. This is the smallest amount of flour shipped in any recent year and contrasts with the high figure of 76 million bushels in 1946-47. The flour exports accounted for 21 percent of total wheat and flour exported from Canada during 1948-49 compared with about 30 percent for each of the two previous seasons. Flour exports in the prewar period (1935-39) were only 13 percent of the total.

Grindings of feed wheat and of the principal coarse grains were also smaller than in 1947-48. Mixed grains, corn, and rye, however, show increased millings, compared with a year earlier.

CANADA: Mill grind of grains, 1948-49,
with comparisons

Month	Wheat for flour	Oats	Barley	Mixed grains	Other grain 1/
	1,000 bushels	1,000 bushels	1,000 bushels	1,000 bushels	1,000 bushels
August............	7,354	1,712	671	1,398	322
September...........	9,811	1,902	673	1,589	299
October............	8,808	1,804	787	1,849	300
November...........	8,617	1,988	921	2,058	334
December...........	7,691	1,710	752	2,010	288
January............	6,524	1,416	785	1,797	358
February...........	6,499	1,394	709	1,750	310
March..............	7,574	1,578	683	1,746	392
April..............	7,028	1,620	711	1,602	416
May................	6,967	1,516	652	1,347	383
June...............	7,373	1,580	634	1,131	448
July...............	6,424	1,193	557	1,015	393
Total............	90,670	19,413	8,535	19,292	4,243
1947-48 total....	109,822	22,980	9,571	18,272	5,112

1/ Includes feed wheat, corn, rye, and buckwheat.

From reports of the Dominion Bureau of Statistics.

FATS AND OILS

PHILIPPINE AUGUST COPRA
EXPORTS LARGEST IN 1949

The following tables show copra and coconut oil exports from the Philippine
Republic during August 1949 with comparisons:

PHILIPPINE REPUBLIC: Copra exports, August 1949 with comparisons
(Long tons)

Country 1/	Copra distribution				
	Average 1935-39	1948 2/	Jan.-Aug. 1949 2/	August 1948 2/	August 1949 2/
United States (total)..	206,801	364,102	207,476	33,094	44,384
Atlantic Coast.....	-	61,618	22,907	4,261	2,226
Gulf Coast.........	-	69,320	26,344	6,746	3,754
Pacific Coast......	-	233,164	158,225	22,087	38,404
Canada.............	-	17,049	7,150	-	2,900
Mexico.............	7,260	-	-	-	-
Panama Canal Zone......	-	707	775	-	-
Panama, Republic of....	-	1,357	209	403	-
Colombia..............	-	6,995	-	300	-
Venezuela.............	-	3,868	1,133	-	-
Austria..............	-	6,000	-	-	-
Belgium..............	10	1,000	2,350	-	600
Denmark..............	6,025	26,536	16,085	-	-
France...............	24,589	65,912	23,757	-	-
Bizonal Germany.......	7,309	17,250	26,560	-	4,560
Italy................	4,079	21,900	9,210	1,100	992
Netherlands..........	28,415	8,949	4,850	2,900	800
Norway...............	91	9,276	8,000	-	1,000
Poland...............	-	31,749	1,500	-	-
Sweden...............	4,183	4,748	7,600	-	-
Switzerland..........	-	1,000	-	-	-
Japan................	1,047	24,339	6,075	-	-
Syria................	-	1,443	700	-	700
Egypt................	1,271	-	-	-	-
Union of South Africa..	-	-	1,996	-	204
Others...............	8,758	11,450	3/ 20,730	-	6,250
Total.............	299,838	625,630	346,156	37,797	62,390

1/ Declared destination. 2/ Preliminary. 3/ 15,850 to Trieste; 2,000 to Algeri;
   2,474 to Palestine; and 406 to others.

American Embassy, Manila.

PHILIPPINE REPUBLIC: Coconut oil exports,
August 1949 with comparisons

Country of destination	Average 1935-39	1948	Jan.-Aug. 1949 1/	August 1948 1/	August 1949 1/
United States....	155,358	41,338	32,246	2,810	5,227
Canada..........	1,885	-	-	-	-
Norway..........	-	-	500	-	-
Bizonal Germany..	660	-	3,830	-	-
Italy...........	-	396	2,188	185	-
Netherlands.....	-	-	915	-	-
China..........	392	-	73	-	73
Hong Kong.......	583	-	-	-	-
Poland.........	-	-	260	-	-
Siam..........	54	-	-	-	-
Trieste........	-	125	-	-	-
Other countries..	2,815	126	517	100	-
Total.......	161,747	41,985	40,529	3,095	5,300

1/ Preliminary.

American Embassy, Manila.

CEYLON COPRA, COCONUT OIL EXPORTS
EXCEED 1948 SHIPMENTS

Ceylon's copra exports during January-June 1949 amounted to 11,729 long tons compared with only 1,284 tons for the comparable period of 1948. Over 68 percent of the total was consigned to European countries.

Coconut oil exports in the first half of 1949 totaled 42,931 tons compared with 37,530 during January-June 1948. The 6-month shipments this year represent almost 73 percent of the 1935-39 average annual exports. Almost 60 percent of the total was sent to the United Kingdom.

At the end of June 1949 the tonnage of coconut oil shipped to the United Kingdom under the terms of the 40,000 ton contract with the Ministry of Food amounted to 25,229 tons. This leaves a balance of nearly 15,000 tons to be shipped during the last half of the year. The estimated amount of coconut oil/copra available for export to other countries during 1949 remains about 50,000 tons, as previously estimated.

Stocks on hand as of June 30, 1949, were 9,800 tons of coconut oil and 219 tons of copra.

Contract prices were unchanged at $181.00 per ton for copra Estate No. 1 and $308.22 for coconut oil, White, wharf delivery.

CEYLON: Copra and coconut oil exports,
January-June 1949 with comparisons
(Long tons)

Country	Copra distribution				Coconut oil distribution			
	Average 1935-39	1948 1/	Jan.-June 1948 1/	Jan.-June 1949 1/	Average 1935-39	1948 1/	Jan.-June 1948 1/	Jan.-June 1949 1/
United States...	1	-	-	-	30	2,362	-	-
Canada..	-	-	-	-	8,523	-	-	-
West Indies....	-	-	-	-	881	-	-	-
Denmark.	1,605	3,395	265	1,197	35	463	-	1,726
France.........	354	287	86	1,100	347	3,418	-	3,657
Germany........	1,482	-	-	-	1,200	-	-	1
Greece.........	1,526	45	45	850	120	5,132	-	3,305
Italy..........	6,541	6,210	100	2,235	1,724	2,424	-	2,583
Netherlands....	-	2,742	-	-	-	-	146	-
Norway.........	150	1,497	-	-	45	100	-	98
Switzerland....	-	3,136	469	2,150	84	52,374	35,715	25,229
United Kingdom.	420	10,757	-	-	14,160	42	-	50
Other Europe...	4,423	1,450	-	500	9,441	223	75	60
Cyprus.........	-	-	250	1,605	146	6,182	1,420	1,723
India..........	42,553	7,604	65	-	10,769	65	40	436
Iraq...........	20	79	-	-	315	2,014	-	3,366
Pakistan.......	-	16,282	-	1,992	-	-	-	-
Palestine......	-	-	-	-	15	110	100	38
Syria.....	60	965	2	100	164	25	-	35
Other Asia.....	360	12	-	-	2,406	47	20	41
Egypt..........	425	-	-	-	2,433	524	-	531
Union of South Africa....	-	-	2	-	2,597	-	-	-
Other countries......	7	-	-	-	3,578	225	14	52
Total......	59,927	54,461	1,284	11,729	59,013	75,730	37,530	42,931

1/ Preliminary.

American Embassy, Colombo.

MALAYA: Copra exports and imports,
January-June 1949 with comparisons
(Long tons)

Country	Copra distribution			
	Average 1935-39	1948 1/	January-June	
			1948 1/	1949 1/
Exports				
Czechoslovakia........	652	600	300	900
Denmark.............	2,050	7,453	3,328	6,032
France.............	8,578	2,196	346	3,490
Italy...............	11,322	8,247	1,549	552
Netherlands.........	28,956	11,323	2,523	2,680
Norway.............	4,703	750	-	4,551
Poland.............	3,358	6,020	-	9,278
Sweden.............	1,850	13,738	9,008	900
United Kingdom......	57,750	2,081	875	-
Other Europe........	49,209	1,480	-	1,030
Morocco............	493	1,873	200	300
Asia...............	3,977	2,664	25	1,120
Other countries.....	18,793	616	-	-
Total...........	191,691	59,041	18,154	30,833
Imports				
British possessions	10,617	5,454	1,305	7,626
Indonesia...........	105,500	81,330	40,979	33,012
Other countries.....	2,134	882	184	543
Total..........	118,251	87,666	42,468	41,181

1/ Preliminary.

American Consulate General, Singapore.

MALAYA: Coconut oil exports and imports,
January-June 1949 with comparisons
(Long tons)

Country	Coconut oil distribution			
	Average 1935-39	1948 1/	January-June	
			1948 1/	1949 1/
Exports				
France................:	100	2,194	1,631	1,336
Italy.................:	20	8,198	2,783	2,312
Netherlands..........:	822	3,488	1,080	1,867
Sweden...............:	185	2,200	2,200	-
United Kingdom.......:	8,857	3,334	3,284	-
Other Europe.........:	290	3,895	1,690	1,925
U.S.S.R. ....:	-	2,700	-	1,000
Burma................:	3,908	3,828	1,520	2,233
Hong Kong............:	1,391	8,031	5,821	1,456
India................:	22,500	299	-	8,558
Indonesia............:	3,119	374	117	425
Iraq.................:	-	937	177	830
Pakistan.............:	-	2,111	-	2,030
Other Asia...........:	1,772	474	225	1,033
Egypt................:	3,295	3,821	2,431	1,856
Other countries......:	850	2,392	1,020	264
Total.......... :	47,109	48,276	23,979	27,125
Imports				
British possessions :	16	174	159	12
Indonesia............:	328	2,857	2,501	109
Other countries......:	229	-	-	-
Total...........:	573	3,031	2,660	121

1/ Preliminary.
American Consulate General, Singapore.

U. S. IMPORTS OF SPECIFIED
VEGETABLE OILS AND OILSEEDS

The following table shows United States imports of specified vegetable oils and oilseeds during January-July 1949 with comparisons:

UNITED STATES: Imports 1/ of specified oils and oilseeds,
January-July 1949 with comparisons

Commodity	Unit	Average 1935-39	1947	1948 2/	January-July	
					1948 2/	1949 2/
Babassu kernels	1,000 lbs.	3/	22,233	61,921	33,161	29,562
Babassu oil	" "	4/ 346	1,747	3,082	1,224	2,112
Castor-beans	" "	132,924	276,807	302,511	168,175	146,925
Castor oil	" "	226	6,595	2,441	1,362	2,791
Flaxseed	" bu.	18,470	282	1,066	928	148
Linseed oil	" lbs.	713	117,326	3,959	3,596	1,310
Copra	Short tons	230,000	677,660	448,862	291,125	192,648
Coconut oil	1,000 lbs.	342,717	23,559	109,096	48,679	57,931
Oiticica oil	" "	4/ 7,673	8,471	17,558	10,726	5,653
Olive oil						
Edible	" "	62,811	11,250	36,101	21,050	10,832
Inedible	" "	35,448	248	9,775	7,371	569
Palm oil	" "	321,482	63,212	63,328	31,102	74,107
Sesame seed	" "	58,425	9,479	22,606	20,301	6,800
Tea-seed oil	" "	13,159	6,377	3,601	3,177	99
Tucum kernels	" "	5/ 9,810	16,887	11,619	11,010	6/ 28,647
Tung oil	" "	123,190	121,564	133,282	74,829	30,992

1/ Imports for consumption. 2/ Preliminary. 3/ Not separately classified in Foreign Commerce and Navigation. 4/ Average of less than 5 years. 5/ 1939 only. 6/ January-June total should read 26,663 as a result of a change in the April figure.

Compiled from official sources.

INDIA ANTICIPATES LARGER PEANUT,
CASTOR, SESAME CROPS

India anticipates increases in the production of peanuts, castor beans, and sesame seed during the 1949-50 season, according to the American Consulate General, Madras.

Peanut production is unofficially forecast at 4,480,000 short tons from about 11,050,000 acres. This is an expansion of 30 percent over the 1948-49 harvest. The increased acreage and the expected increased production of the primary peanut crop result from the absence of statutory control over the prices of oilseeds as against the Government controlled rates for food grains and cotton, and from the prevalence of ideal weather conditions. The acreage and production of the secondary crop were reduced by lack of rains and the resultant insufficient water supply for irrigation.

Unofficial sources forecast a castor bean harvest of 128,800 tons from 1,500,000 acres, compared with 122,000 tons from 1,406,000 acres in 1948-49. A larger-than-usual area is expected to be brought under castor cultivation in Hyderabad.

Sesame seed is forecast at 403,200 tons and 3,750,000 acres against 330,400 tons and 3,567,000 acres in 1948-49. Increased cultivation in Hyderabad is also anticipated for this crop. Exports of sesame continue to be banned. The entire production is utilized domestically in the form of oil.

VEGETABLE OILSEEDS AND OILS
SITUATION IN GUATEMALA

Guatemala will produce approximately 2.3 million pounds of vegetable oils during the crop year beginning November 1, 1948, and ending October 31, 1949, according to the American Embassy, Guatemala. The total will include 1 million pounds of oil from Native palms (indiscriminately referred to as "corozo"), 900 thousand pounds of sesame oil, 300 thousand pounds of cottonseed oil, and 100 thousand pounds of miscellaneous oils including castor, coconut, and peanut oil.

Corozo palms grow wild, and few if any are under cultivation. Commercial collection of the fruit is practiced only where adequate labor and transportation are available. Most of the nuts are hand-cracked by the collectors, although a few shelling machines are in use. Coconut oil is occasionally extracted from native copra, but the quantity is small in comparison with corozo. A large fruit company maintains plantings of 1,600 acres of African oil palms which will begin bearing commercially next year. Oil extraction equipment will be installed in the near future.

The sesame crop for 1948 (harvested last November and December) probably produced in the neighborhood of 4 million pounds of seed, and is considered one of the largest to be harvested in Guatemala. On the basis of an estimated mean yield of 500 pounds to the acre, harvested acreage would thus be 8,000 acres. Most of the crop was grown by small farmers using simple hand methods. Approximately 300,000 pounds of cottonseed oil was produced in 1948. Much of the castor oil is obtained from wild beans, and peanut plantings in Guatemala probably total no more than 1,000 acres with an estimated output of 500,000 pounds of nuts in the shells, relatively few of which are crushed for oil.

A new, excellently equiped oilseed crushing plant has been operating on a trial basis since about August 1. With a capacity of about 3.6 million pounds of oil annually, it will soon go into full-scale production of refined oils and shortening, utilizing cottonseed, sesame, and corozo. Three other crushers are now operating, one of which will produce only castor oil with the advent of the new plant mentioned above. These 4 plants are in Guatemala City. A plant at Mazatenango, which was an important crusher of cottonseed, was reportedly severely damaged by fire and is now installing new equipment.

The market for all fats and oils has weakened in Guatemala during the last six months. Imports are increasing and interest in domestic fats is declining. Decision of the Guatemalan Government to lift its export embargo on sesame seed was an indication of the weakening of the domestic market.

According to present indications, production of seed from the sesame crop to be harvested in November and December 1949, will be materially less than was that from the 1948 crop. Crushers, who during the last few years advanced money to finance growers, are not doing so this year and growers may prove dissatisfied with prices received for this year's crop.

Cottonseed is expected to be available in greater quantity this year than last since this year's cotton crop will be somewhat larger than that of 1948. New gins and crushing facilities also probably will bring about the milling of a higher percentage of the country's supply of cottonseed than in 1948-49 and previously.

Gathering of wild corozo nuts will continue to be determined largely by alternative opportunities of employment for residents of the Caribbean Lowlands and the Peten. Various circumstances have seriously reduced the income derived from the lumbering and chicle gathering industries, and until these industries revive, or others are established, workers will collect and prepare palm nuts.

TROPICAL PRODUCTS

INDONESIA'S PEPPER PRODUCTION
CONTINUES LOW

Indonesia's 1949 pepper output is estimated at 11 million pounds, according to the American Consulate General in Batavia. This compares with 11 million pounds in 1948 and an annual average prewar (1935-39) production of 135 million pounds.

Pepper prices in Indonesia when converted to dollars at the official exchange rate are substantially higher than quotations in the United States. At a recent auction in Batavia, 25 tons of black pepper were sold for the equivalent of $1.80 per pound, cost and freight, New York as compared with the New York wholesale price of $1.35 per pound.   From 2 to 3 million pounds of Lampong black pepper will be offered for sale in September and October 1949. European buyers are expected to get most of these offerings because of price considerations and less strict sanitation requirements.

Most of Indonesia's supplies of black pepper from previous crops are exhausted, and, as a consequence, the quality of offerings is expected to improve. Old stocks of white pepper on Banka are estimated at more than 2 million pounds.

Before the war, Indonesia was the source of about 85 percent of the world's pepper supply. The Lampong District of South Sumatra accounted for about 70 percent of the Islands' total production, Banka 20 percent, and Borneo, Acheen, and Java the remaining 10 percent.

During the occupation, the Japanese ordered extensive areas of pepper vines uprooted to make way for food and fiber crops. In Banka, the center of white pepper production, the pepper industry was almost completely destroyed. Of the 12 million vines cultivated there before the war, only 174 thousand remained on VJ Day. In the Lampong District, chief source of black pepper in Indonesia, it is estimated that the acreage lost through destruction and neglect amounted to about two-thirds of the prewar area. In Borneo, very little of the prewar acreage was left.

At present, Banka has about 600,000 pepper vines. It will take many years to reestablish Banka as an important pepper producing area. Much work is involved, and the cost of labor is high. Rehabilitation of the pepper industry in Borneo is progressing very slowly. The outlook for the Lampong District, however, is relatively encouraging. Production is now more than 10 percent of the prewar average and is expected to rise sharply when security conditions prevail.

SLIGHTLY SMALLER NIGERIAN CACAO
PRODUCTION FORECAST FOR 1949-50

Nigeria's 1949-50 cacao output has been tentatively forecast at around 225 million pounds, according to the American Consulate General in Lagos. This compares with 240 million pounds in 1948-49, 166 million pounds in 1947-48, and an annual average prewar (1935-39) production of 216 million pounds.

So far, weather conditions have been favorable, and harvesting of the 1949-50 main crop is expected to begin during the last week in September. Much can still happen in the next few months to reduce the size of the harvest.

Swollen Shoot, the most serious disease affecting Nigeria's cacao trees, has suddenly broken out in new areas. Last March, the Cocoa Survey Department stated that this disease would be virtually eliminated with the removal of another 200,000 trees. This quantity was cut out, making a total removed of 800,000 of Nigeria's 200 million cacao trees. However, a new outbreak was recently discovered affecting at least 600,000 more trees. In an effort to check the new outbreak, 5 agricultural officers have been added to the inspection force and the Nigeria Cocoa Marketing Board has undertaken the additional expense of $250,000.

The Nigeria Cocoa Marketing Board has announced new substantially reduced prices it will pay to producers for the 1949-50 cacao crop. These prices are given in the following table, together with the equivalent in cents per pound and comparable prices for the 1948-49 season:

GRADES	1948-49		1949-50	
	British Pounds per ton	Cents per pound	British Pounds per ton	Cents per pound
Main Crop				
1	120	21.6	100	18.0
2	115	20.7	95	17.1
3	105	18.9	75	13.5
Mid Crop				
1	115	20.7	95	17.1
2	110	19.8	90	16.2
3	100	18.0	70	12.6

COTTON AND OTHER FIBER

COTTON-PRICE QUOTATIONS
ON FOREIGN MARKETS

The following table shows certain cotton-price quotations on foreign markets converted at current rates of exchange.

COTTON: Spot prices in certain foreign markets, and the U.S. gulf-port average

Market location, kind, and quality	Date 1949	Unit of weight	Unit of currency	Price in foreign currency	Equivalent U.S. cents per pound
Alexandria		Kantar			
Ashmouni, Good..........	9-15	99.05 lbs.	Tallari	50.50	42.10
Ashmouni, F.G.F.........	"	"	"	48.50	40.43
Karnak, Good............	"	"	"	(not quoted)	
Karnak, F.G.F...........	"	"	"	(not quoted)	
Bombay		Candy			
Jarila, Fine............	9-15	784 lbs.	Rupee	620.00	23.86
Broach Vijay, Fine......	"	"	"	1/ 690.00	26.55
Karachi		Maund			
4F Punjab, S.G., Fine...	9-14	82.28 lbs.	"	84.00	30.80
289F Sind, S.G., Fine...	"	"	"	89.00	32.63
289F Punjab, S.G., Fine.	"	"	"	90.00	33.00
Buenos Aires		Metric ton			
Type B.................	9-15	2204.6 lbs.	Peso	1/ 4000.00	54.03
Lima		Sp. quintal			
Tanguis, Type 5.........	9-14	101.4 lbs.	Sol	400.00	38.70
Pima, Type 1............	"	"	"	480.00	46.44
Recife		Arroba			
Mata, Type 4............	9-15	33.07 lbs.	Cruzeiro	210.00	34.55
Sertao, Type 5..........	"	"	"	210.00	34.55
Sao Paulo					
Sao Paulo, Type 5.......	9-15	"	"	206.00	33.89
Torreon		Sp. quintal			
Middling, 15/16"........	9-14	101.4 lbs.	Peso	201.00	22.94
Houston-Galveston-New					
Orleans av. Mid. 15/16".	9-15	Pound	Cent	XXXXX	29.67

Quotations of foreign markets reported by cable from U.S. Foreign Service posts abroad. U. S. quotations from designated spot markets.

1/ Nominal.

FRUITS, VEGETABLES AND NUTS

CANADIAN FRUIT
ESTIMATE REVISED

The third estimate of fruit production in Canada places the apple crop at 16,341,000 bushels, 22 percent higher than the 1948 crop of 13,404,000 and 11 percent above the prewar average of 14,560,000 bushels. Increases are indicated in all provinces except New Brunswick, estimated at 300,000 bushels.

Production and percents of increase in other provinces are as follows: Nova Scotia, 3,600,000, 57 percent; Ontario, 3,021,000, 29 percent; Quebec, 1,500,000, 25 percent and British Columbia, 7,920,000, 9 percent. Pear production, estimated at 938,000 bushels is an increase of 19 percent over the previous year's crop of 789,000 and 65 percent higher than the prewar average of 569,000. The plum and prune crop indicated to be 19,500 tons is an increase of 16 percent over the 1948 crop of 16,775 and 3 times as many as were produced prewar. Peaches, indicated at 1,993,000 bushels are 10 percent above the previous year's crop of 1,760,000 and are the largest crop since 1946 when 2,145,000 were produced.

The cherry and apricot crops estimated at 11,025 and 4,575 short tons respectively are both increases over the 1948 crops of 9,800 and 3,800 short tons.

L A T E   N E W S

Cuban rice arrivals from January through September 8 totaled 298 million pounds, according to ships' manifests. All except 1 million pounds of this quantity reportedly originated in the United States. On this basis, under the Cuban tariff quota of 451 million pounds, 153 million pounds may yet be imported, nearly one-third of which reportedly has been purchased and is expected to arrive in mid-October.

- - - - - -

The Government of Switzerland in Ordinance No. 59, which went into effect on August 18, 1949, abolished all forms of rationing, both direct and indirect, for flour, rice and edible fats and oils.

CPSIA information can be obtained
at www.ICGtesting.com
Printed in the USA
BVHW090435201118
533516BV00014B/909/P

9 781528 392228